This Planner Belongs To:

A Look At
My Assets & Liabilities

YEARLY FINANCIAL *Goals*

THIS YEAR *my primary goals are*

JAN

FEB

MAR

APR

MAY

JUN

JUL

AUG

SEP

OCT

NOV

DEC

BALANCE *Sheet*

DATE:

CREDIT SCORE:

NET WORTH:

FINANCIALS

LIABILITIES: **ASSETS:**

ASSETS	AMOUNT	LIABILITIES	AMOUNT
CASH		**DEBTS**	
		SUBTOTAL:	
INVESTMENTS			
SUBTOTAL:		**LOANS**	
		SUBTOTAL:	
REAL ESTATE		**MORTGAGE**	
SUBTOTAL:			
		SUBTOTAL:	
OTHER		**OTHER**	
SUBTOTAL:		SUBTOTAL:	

DEBT REPAYMENT *Plan*

ACCOUNT:

WEBSITE URL:

PRIORITY#

COMPANY:

CREDIT TYPE:

CREDIT LIMIT:

USERNAME: PASSWORD:

GOAL PAYOFF DATE

STARTING BALANCE:

INTEREST ACCRUED: DUE DATE:

PAYMENT DATE	PAYMENT AMOUNT	CURRENT BALANCE

DEBT REPAYMENT *Plan*

ACCOUNT: **WEBSITE URL:**

PRIORITY#

COMPANY: USERNAME: PASSWORD:

CREDIT TYPE:

CREDIT LIMIT: **STARTING BALANCE:**

GOAL PAYOFF DATE

INTEREST ACCRUED: DUE DATE:

PAYMENT DATE   **PAYMENT AMOUNT**   **CURRENT BALANCE**

ACCOUNT *Tracker*

ACCOUNT # 1

FINANCIAL INSTITUTION:

ACCOUNT #:

NAME ON ACCOUNT:

ACCOUNT TYPE:

CARD NUMBER:

ROUTING/TRANSIT #:

OTHER:

NOTES

ACCOUNT # 2

FINANCIAL INSTITUTION:

ACCOUNT #:

NAME ON ACCOUNT:

ACCOUNT TYPE:

CARD NUMBER:

ROUTING/TRANSIT #:

OTHER:

NOTES

ACCOUNT # 3

FINANCIAL INSTITUTION:

ACCOUNT #:

NAME ON ACCOUNT:

ACCOUNT TYPE:

CARD NUMBER:

ROUTING/TRANSIT #:

OTHER:

NOTES

AUTO REPAIR *Tracker*

CAR MAKE: **YEAR:**

CAR MODEL: **VIN #:**

DATE	REPAIR	COST

HOME REPAIR *Tracker*

YEAR:

DATE	REPAIR	COST

MY TRAVEL *Budget*

BUDGET BREAKDOWN: **TRAVEL NOTES:**

PLANE TICKETS**:**

TRANSPORTATION:

LODGING:

FOOD/SHOPPING: **TOTALS:**

GOAL PAYOFF DATE

TOTAL COST OF TRIP: AMOUNT TO RAISE:

PAYMENT DATE   **PAYMENT AMOUNT**   **CURRENT BALANCE**

TRAVEL *Contacts*

LOCATION:

HOTEL:

ADDRESS #:

PHONE#:

WEBSITE URL:

AMOUNT PER NIGHT::

RESERVATION INFORMATION:

DUE DATE:

ROOM DETAILS:

BILL TOTAL:

HOTEL:

ACCOUNT #:

PHONE#:

WEBSITE URL:

AMOUNT PER NIGHT::

RESERVATION INFORMATION:

DUE DATE:

ROOM DETAILS:

BILL TOTAL:

HOTEL:

ACCOUNT #:

PHONE#:

WEBSITE URL:

AMOUNT PER NIGHT:

RESERVATION INFORMATION:

DUE DATE:

ROOM DETAILS:

BILL TOTAL:

NOTES

TRAVEL *Contacts*

LOCATION:

CAR RENTAL:

ADDRESS #:   WEBSITE URL:

PHONE#:   AMOUNT PER NIGHT::

RESERVATION INFORMATION: **DUE DATE:**   **CAR DETAILS:**

BILL TOTAL:

CAR RENTAL:

ACCOUNT #:   WEBSITE URL:

PHONE#:   AMOUNT PER NIGHT::

RESERVATION INFORMATION: **DUE DATE:**   **CAR DETAILS:**

BILL TOTAL:

TRAIN PASS:

ACCOUNT #:   WEBSITE URL:

PHONE#:   AMOUNT PER NIGHT:

RESERVATION INFORMATION: **DUE DATE:**   **PASS DETAILS:**

BILL TOTAL:

NOTES

TRAVEL *Contacts*

LOCATION:

TRAIN PASS:

ADDRESS #:

WEBSITE URL:

PHONE#:

AMOUNT PER NIGHT::

RESERVATION INFORMATION: DUE DATE: TRAIN DETAILS:

BILL TOTAL:

AIRPLANE TICKETS:

AIRLINE:

WEBSITE URL:

PHONE #:

AMOUNT PER SEAT::

RESERVATION INFORMATION: DUE DATE: FLIGHT DETAILS:

BILL TOTAL:

EVENT TICKETS:

EVENT:

WEBSITE URL:

PHONE#:

AMOUNT PER TICKET:

RESERVATION INFORMATION: DUE DATE: EVENT DETAILS:

BILL TOTAL:

NOTES

Planning My Monthly Budget

RECURRING *Bills*

FREQUENCY:

COMPANY:

ACCOUNT #:

PHONE#:

WEBSITE URL:

BILL DUE DATE:

ONLINE ACCOUNT INFORMATION: **USERNAME**   **PASSWORD**

BILL TOTAL:

COMPANY:

ACCOUNT #:

PHONE#:

WEBSITE URL:

BILL DUE DATE:

ONLINE ACCOUNT INFORMATION: **USERNAME**   **PASSWORD**

BILL TOTAL:

COMPANY:

ACCOUNT #:

PHONE#:

WEBSITE URL:

BILL DUE DATE:

ONLINE ACCOUNT INFORMATION: **USERNAME**   **PASSWORD**

BILL TOTAL:

NOTES

RECURRING *Bills*

FREQUENCY:

COMPANY:

ACCOUNT #:   WEBSITE URL:

PHONE#:   BILL DUE DATE:

ONLINE ACCOUNT INFORMATION: **USERNAME**   **PASSWORD**

BILL TOTAL:

COMPANY:

ACCOUNT #:   WEBSITE URL:

PHONE#:   BILL DUE DATE:

ONLINE ACCOUNT INFORMATION: **USERNAME**   **PASSWORD**

BILL TOTAL:

COMPANY:

ACCOUNT #:   WEBSITE URL:

PHONE#:   BILL DUE DATE:

ONLINE ACCOUNT INFORMATION: **USERNAME**   **PASSWORD**

BILL TOTAL:

NOTES

RECURRING *Bills*

FREQUENCY:

COMPANY:

ACCOUNT #:   WEBSITE URL:

PHONE#:   BILL DUE DATE:

ONLINE ACCOUNT INFORMATION: **USERNAME**   **PASSWORD**

BILL TOTAL:

COMPANY:

ACCOUNT #:   WEBSITE URL:

PHONE#:   BILL DUE DATE:

ONLINE ACCOUNT INFORMATION: **USERNAME**   **PASSWORD**

BILL TOTAL:

COMPANY:

ACCOUNT #:   WEBSITE URL:

PHONE#:   BILL DUE DATE:

ONLINE ACCOUNT INFORMATION: **USERNAME**   **PASSWORD**

BILL TOTAL:

NOTES

RECURRING *Bills*

FREQUENCY:

COMPANY:

ACCOUNT #:
PHONE#:

WEBSITE URL:
BILL DUE DATE:

ONLINE ACCOUNT INFORMATION: **USERNAME**   **PASSWORD**

BILL TOTAL:

COMPANY:

ACCOUNT #:
PHONE#:

WEBSITE URL:
BILL DUE DATE:

ONLINE ACCOUNT INFORMATION: **USERNAME**   **PASSWORD**

BILL TOTAL:

COMPANY:

ACCOUNT #:
PHONE#:

WEBSITE URL:
BILL DUE DATE:

ONLINE ACCOUNT INFORMATION: **USERNAME**   **PASSWORD**

BILL TOTAL:

NOTES

INCOME *Tracker*

- MONTHLY -

SOURCE	AMOUNT	M	T	W	T	F	S	S

MONTHLY 

MONTHLY INCOME: **BUDGETED:**   **ACTUAL COST:**   **DIFFERENCE:**

Household Utilities/Expenses

SUBTOTAL: **% OF INCOME:**

Debt/Payments/Travel Budget

SUBTOTAL: **% OF INCOME:**

Personal/Other

SUBTOTAL: **% OF INCOME:**

MONTHLY EXPENSE *Tracker*

MONTH:

GROCERIES

DATE	ITEM	AMOUNT

HOME

DATE	ITEM	AMOUNT

PERSONAL

DATE	ITEM	AMOUNT

ACTIVITIES

DATE	ITEM	AMOUNT

RECREATION

DATE	ITEM	AMOUNT

MISC

DATE	ITEM	AMOUNT

Goal Setting
& Daily Spending Actuals

MONTH 1

Date:_______________________

INCOME *Tracker*
- MONTHLY -

SOURCE	AMOUNT	M	T	W	T	F	S	S

ONE-TIME *Bills*

MONTH:

COMPANY:

ACCOUNT #:

WEBSITE URL:

PHONE#:

BILL DUE DATE:

ONLINE ACCOUNT INFORMATION: **USERNAME** **PASSWORD**

BILL TOTAL:

COMPANY:

ACCOUNT #:

WEBSITE URL:

PHONE#:

BILL DUE DATE:

ONLINE ACCOUNT INFORMATION: **USERNAME** **PASSWORD**

BILL TOTAL:

COMPANY:

ACCOUNT #:

WEBSITE URL:

PHONE#:

BILL DUE DATE:

ONLINE ACCOUNT INFORMATION: **USERNAME** **PASSWORD**

BILL TOTAL:

NOTES

INCOME *Tracker*
- MONTHLY -

SOURCE	AMOUNT	M	T	W	T	F	S	S

ONE-TIME *Bills*

MONTH:

COMPANY:

ACCOUNT #:

PHONE#:

WEBSITE URL:

BILL DUE DATE:

ONLINE ACCOUNT INFORMATION: **USERNAME** **PASSWORD**

BILL TOTAL:

COMPANY:

ACCOUNT #:

PHONE#:

WEBSITE URL:

BILL DUE DATE:

ONLINE ACCOUNT INFORMATION: **USERNAME** **PASSWORD**

BILL TOTAL:

COMPANY:

ACCOUNT #:

PHONE#:

WEBSITE URL:

BILL DUE DATE:

ONLINE ACCOUNT INFORMATION: **USERNAME** **PASSWORD**

BILL TOTAL:

NOTES

ONE-TIME *Bills*

MONTH:

COMPANY:

ACCOUNT #:

PHONE#:

WEBSITE URL:

BILL DUE DATE:

ONLINE ACCOUNT INFORMATION: **USERNAME** **PASSWORD**

BILL TOTAL:

COMPANY:

ACCOUNT #:

PHONE#:

WEBSITE URL:

BILL DUE DATE:

ONLINE ACCOUNT INFORMATION: **USERNAME** **PASSWORD**

BILL TOTAL:

COMPANY:

ACCOUNT #:

PHONE#:

WEBSITE URL:

BILL DUE DATE:

ONLINE ACCOUNT INFORMATION: **USERNAME** **PASSWORD**

BILL TOTAL:

NOTES

WEEKLY EXPENSE *Tracker*

DATES:

DESCRIPTION	CATEGORY	COST	NEED	WANT

DAILY LIFE *Planner*

DATES:

TODAY, *my primary goals are*

MOR

AFT

EVE

TODAY, *my primary goals are*

MOR

AFT

EVE

TODAY, *my primary goals are*

MOR

AFT

EVE

DAILY LIFE *Planner*

DATES:

TODAY, *my primary goals are*

MOR

AFT

EVE

TODAY, *my primary goals are*

MOR

AFT

EVE

TODAY, *my primary goals are*

MOR

AFT

EVE

DAILY LIFE *Planner*

DATES:

TODAY, *my primary goals are*

MOR

AFT

EVE

NOTES:

WEEKLY EXPENSE *Tracker*

DATES:

DESCRIPTION	CATEGORY	COST	NEED	WANT

DAILY LIFE *Planner*

DATES:

TODAY, *my primary goals are*

MOR

AFT

EVE

TODAY, *my primary goals are*

MOR

AFT

EVE

TODAY, *my primary goals are*

MOR

AFT

EVE

DAILY LIFE *Planner*

DATES:

TODAY, *my primary goals are*

(MOR)　　　　(AFT)　　　　(EVE)

TODAY, *my primary goals are*

(MOR)　　　　(AFT)　　　　(EVE)

TODAY, *my primary goals are*

(MOR)　　　　(AFT)　　　　(EVE)

DAILY LIFE *Planner*

DATES:

TODAY, *my primary goals are*

MOR

AFT

EVE

NOTES:

WEEKLY EXPENSE *Tracker*

DATES:

DESCRIPTION	CATEGORY	COST		NEED	WANT

DAILY LIFE *Planner*

DATES:

TODAY, *my primary goals are*

MOR

AFT

EVE

TODAY, *my primary goals are*

MOR

AFT

EVE

TODAY, *my primary goals are*

MOR

AFT

EVE

DAILY LIFE *Planner*

DATES:

TODAY, *my primary goals are*

(MOR)   (AFT)   (EVE)

TODAY, *my primary goals are*

(MOR)   (AFT)   (EVE)

TODAY, *my primary goals are*

(MOR)   (AFT)   (EVE)

DAILY LIFE *Planner*

DATES:

TODAY, *my primary goals are*

MOR	AFT	EVE

NOTES:

WEEKLY EXPENSE *Tracker*

DATES:

DESCRIPTION	CATEGORY	COST	NEED	WANT

DAILY LIFE *Planner*

DATES:

TODAY, *my primary goals are*

MOR   **AFT**   **EVE**

TODAY, *my primary goals are*

MOR   **AFT**   **EVE**

TODAY, *my primary goals are*

MOR   **AFT**   **EVE**

DAILY LIFE *Planner*

DATES:

TODAY, *my primary goals are*

MOR

AFT

EVE

TODAY, *my primary goals are*

MOR

AFT

EVE

TODAY, *my primary goals are*

MOR

AFT

EVE

DAILY LIFE *Planner*

DATES:

TODAY, *my primary goals are*

MOR　　　　　　　　**AFT**　　　　　　　　**EVE**

NOTES:

FINANCIAL *Journal*

MONTH 2

Date:_______________________

INCOME *Tracker*

- MONTHLY -

SOURCE	AMOUNT	M	T	W	T	F	S	S

ONE-TIME *Bills*

MONTH:

COMPANY:

ACCOUNT #: WEBSITE URL:

PHONE#: BILL DUE DATE:

ONLINE ACCOUNT INFORMATION: **USERNAME** **PASSWORD**

BILL TOTAL:

COMPANY:

ACCOUNT #: WEBSITE URL:

PHONE#: BILL DUE DATE:

ONLINE ACCOUNT INFORMATION: **USERNAME** **PASSWORD**

BILL TOTAL:

COMPANY:

ACCOUNT #: WEBSITE URL:

PHONE#: BILL DUE DATE:

ONLINE ACCOUNT INFORMATION: **USERNAME** **PASSWORD**

BILL TOTAL:

NOTES

ONE-TIME *Bills*

MONTH:

COMPANY:

ACCOUNT #:

PHONE#:

WEBSITE URL:

BILL DUE DATE:

ONLINE ACCOUNT INFORMATION: **USERNAME**   **PASSWORD**

BILL TOTAL:

COMPANY:

ACCOUNT #:

PHONE#:

WEBSITE URL:

BILL DUE DATE:

ONLINE ACCOUNT INFORMATION: **USERNAME**   **PASSWORD**

BILL TOTAL:

COMPANY:

ACCOUNT #:

PHONE#:

WEBSITE URL:

BILL DUE DATE:

ONLINE ACCOUNT INFORMATION: **USERNAME**   **PASSWORD**

BILL TOTAL:

NOTES

WEEKLY EXPENSE *Tracker*

DATES:

DESCRIPTION	CATEGORY	COST	NEED	WANT

DAILY LIFE *Planner*

DATES:

TODAY, *my primary goals are*

(MOR)　　　　　(AFT)　　　　　(EVE)

TODAY, *my primary goals are*

(MOR)　　　　　(AFT)　　　　　(EVE)

TODAY, *my primary goals are*

(MOR)　　　　　(AFT)　　　　　(EVE)

DAILY LIFE *Planner*

DATES:

TODAY, *my primary goals are*

MOR

AFT

EVE

TODAY, *my primary goals are*

MOR

AFT

EVE

TODAY, *my primary goals are*

MOR

AFT

EVE

DAILY LIFE *Planner*

DATES:

TODAY, *my primary goals are*

MOR

AFT

EVE

NOTES:

WEEKLY EXPENSE *Tracker*

DATES:

DESCRIPTION	CATEGORY	COST	NEED	WANT

DAILY LIFE *Planner*

DATES:

TODAY, *my primary goals are*

MOR

AFT

EVE

TODAY, *my primary goals are*

MOR

AFT

EVE

TODAY, *my primary goals are*

MOR

AFT

EVE

DAILY LIFE *Planner*

DATES:

TODAY, *my primary goals are*

MOR

AFT

EVE

TODAY, *my primary goals are*

MOR

AFT

EVE

TODAY, *my primary goals are*

MOR

AFT

EVE

DAILY LIFE *Planner*

DATES:

TODAY, *my primary goals are*

MOR

AFT

EVE

NOTES:

WEEKLY EXPENSE *Tracker*

DATES:

DESCRIPTION	CATEGORY	COST	NEED	WANT

DAILY LIFE *Planner*

DATES:

TODAY, *my primary goals are*

MOR

AFT

EVE

TODAY, *my primary goals are*

MOR

AFT

EVE

TODAY, *my primary goals are*

MOR

AFT

EVE

DAILY LIFE *Planner*

DATES:

TODAY, *my primary goals are*

MOR

AFT

EVE

TODAY, *my primary goals are*

MOR

AFT

EVE

TODAY, *my primary goals are*

MOR

AFT

EVE

DAILY LIFE *Planner*

DATES:

TODAY, *my primary goals are*

MOR

AFT

EVE

NOTES:

WEEKLY EXPENSE *Tracker*

DATES:

DESCRIPTION	CATEGORY	COST	NEED	WANT

DAILY LIFE *Planner*

DATES:

TODAY, *my primary goals are*

MOR

AFT

EVE

____

____

____

TODAY, *my primary goals are*

MOR

AFT

EVE

____

____

____

TODAY, *my primary goals are*

MOR

AFT

EVE

____

____

____

DAILY LIFE *Planner*

DATES:

TODAY, *my primary goals are*

MOR

AFT

EVE

TODAY, *my primary goals are*

MOR

AFT

EVE

TODAY, *my primary goals are*

MOR

AFT

EVE

DAILY LIFE *Planner*

DATES:

TODAY, *my primary goals are*

MOR

AFT

EVE

NOTES:

FINANCIAL *Journal*

MONTH 3

Date:_________________

INCOME *Tracker*
- MONTHLY -

SOURCE	AMOUNT	M	T	W	T	F	S	S

ONE-TIME *Bills*

MONTH:

COMPANY:

ACCOUNT #:

PHONE#:

WEBSITE URL:

BILL DUE DATE:

ONLINE ACCOUNT INFORMATION: **USERNAME**   **PASSWORD**

BILL TOTAL:

COMPANY:

ACCOUNT #:

PHONE#:

WEBSITE URL:

BILL DUE DATE:

ONLINE ACCOUNT INFORMATION: **USERNAME**   **PASSWORD**

BILL TOTAL:

COMPANY:

ACCOUNT #:

PHONE#:

WEBSITE URL:

BILL DUE DATE:

ONLINE ACCOUNT INFORMATION: **USERNAME**   **PASSWORD**

BILL TOTAL:

NOTES

ONE-TIME *Bills*

MONTH:

COMPANY:

ACCOUNT #:   WEBSITE URL:

PHONE#:   BILL DUE DATE:

ONLINE ACCOUNT INFORMATION: **USERNAME**   **PASSWORD**

BILL TOTAL:

COMPANY:

ACCOUNT #:   WEBSITE URL:

PHONE#:   BILL DUE DATE:

ONLINE ACCOUNT INFORMATION: **USERNAME**   **PASSWORD**

BILL TOTAL:

COMPANY:

ACCOUNT #:   WEBSITE URL:

PHONE#:   BILL DUE DATE:

ONLINE ACCOUNT INFORMATION: **USERNAME**   **PASSWORD**

BILL TOTAL:

NOTES

WEEKLY EXPENSE *Tracker*

DATES:

DESCRIPTION	CATEGORY	COST	NEED	WANT

DAILY LIFE *Planner*

DATES:

TODAY, *my primary goals are*

MOR

AFT

EVE

TODAY, *my primary goals are*

MOR

AFT

EVE

TODAY, *my primary goals are*

MOR

AFT

EVE

DAILY LIFE *Planner*

DATES:

TODAY, *my primary goals are*

MOR

AFT

EVE

TODAY, *my primary goals are*

MOR

AFT

EVE

TODAY, *my primary goals are*

MOR

AFT

EVE

DAILY LIFE *Planner*

DATES:

TODAY, *my primary goals are*

MOR

AFT

EVE

NOTES:

WEEKLY EXPENSE *Tracker*

DATES:

DESCRIPTION	CATEGORY	COST	NEED	WANT

DAILY LIFE *Planner*

DATES:

TODAY, *my primary goals are*

MOR

AFT

EVE

TODAY, *my primary goals are*

MOR

AFT

EVE

TODAY, *my primary goals are*

MOR

AFT

EVE

DAILY LIFE *Planner*

DATES:

TODAY, *my primary goals are*

MOR

AFT

EVE

TODAY, *my primary goals are*

MOR

AFT

EVE

TODAY, *my primary goals are*

MOR

AFT

EVE

DAILY LIFE *Planner*

DATES:

TODAY, *my primary goals are*

MOR

AFT

EVE

NOTES:

WEEKLY EXPENSE *Tracker*

DATES:

DESCRIPTION	CATEGORY	COST	NEED	WANT

DAILY LIFE *Planner*

DATES:

TODAY, *my primary goals are*

MOR

AFT

EVE

TODAY, *my primary goals are*

MOR

AFT

EVE

TODAY, *my primary goals are*

MOR

AFT

EVE

DAILY LIFE *Planner*

DATES:

TODAY, *my primary goals are*

MOR

AFT

EVE

TODAY, *my primary goals are*

MOR

AFT

EVE

TODAY, *my primary goals are*

MOR

AFT

EVE

DAILY LIFE *Planner*

DATES:

TODAY, *my primary goals are*

MOR	AFT	EVE

NOTES:

WEEKLY EXPENSE *Tracker*

DATES:

DESCRIPTION	CATEGORY	COST	NEED	WANT

DAILY LIFE *Planner*

DATES:

TODAY, *my primary goals are*

MOR

AFT

EVE

TODAY, *my primary goals are*

MOR

AFT

EVE

TODAY, *my primary goals are*

MOR

AFT

EVE

DAILY LIFE *Planner*

DATES:

TODAY, *my primary goals are*

MOR

AFT

EVE

TODAY, *my primary goals are*

MOR

AFT

EVE

TODAY, *my primary goals are*

MOR

AFT

EVE

DAILY LIFE *Planner*

DATES:

TODAY, *my primary goals are*

MOR

AFT

EVE

NOTES:

FINANCIAL *Journal*

DAILY LIFE *Planner*

DATES:

TODAY, *my primary goals are*

MOR

AFT

EVE

NOTES:

FINANCIAL *Journal*

MONTH 4

Date:_______________________

INCOME *Tracker*

- MONTHLY -

SOURCE	AMOUNT	M	T	W	T	F	S	S

ONE-TIME *Bills*

MONTH:

COMPANY:

ACCOUNT #:   WEBSITE URL:

PHONE#:   BILL DUE DATE:

ONLINE ACCOUNT INFORMATION: **USERNAME**   **PASSWORD**

BILL TOTAL:

COMPANY:

ACCOUNT #:   WEBSITE URL:

PHONE#:   BILL DUE DATE:

ONLINE ACCOUNT INFORMATION: **USERNAME**   **PASSWORD**

BILL TOTAL:

COMPANY:

ACCOUNT #:   WEBSITE URL:

PHONE#:   BILL DUE DATE:

ONLINE ACCOUNT INFORMATION: **USERNAME**   **PASSWORD**

BILL TOTAL:

NOTES

ONE-TIME *Bills*

MONTH:

COMPANY:

ACCOUNT #:

PHONE#:

WEBSITE URL:

BILL DUE DATE:

ONLINE ACCOUNT INFORMATION: **USERNAME**   **PASSWORD**

BILL TOTAL:

COMPANY:

ACCOUNT #:

PHONE#:

WEBSITE URL:

BILL DUE DATE:

ONLINE ACCOUNT INFORMATION: **USERNAME**   **PASSWORD**

BILL TOTAL:

COMPANY:

ACCOUNT #:

PHONE#:

WEBSITE URL:

BILL DUE DATE:

ONLINE ACCOUNT INFORMATION: **USERNAME**   **PASSWORD**

BILL TOTAL:

NOTES

WEEKLY EXPENSE *Tracker*

DATES:

DESCRIPTION	CATEGORY	COST	NEED	WANT

DAILY LIFE *Planner*

DATES:

TODAY, *my primary goals are*

MOR

AFT

EVE

TODAY, *my primary goals are*

MOR

AFT

EVE

TODAY, *my primary goals are*

MOR

AFT

EVE

DAILY LIFE *Planner*

DATES:

TODAY, *my primary goals are*

MOR   **AFT**   **EVE**

TODAY, *my primary goals are*

MOR   **AFT**   **EVE**

TODAY, *my primary goals are*

MOR   **AFT**   **EVE**

DAILY LIFE *Planner*

DATES:

TODAY, *my primary goals are*

MOR

AFT

EVE

NOTES:

WEEKLY EXPENSE *Tracker*

DATES:

DESCRIPTION	CATEGORY	COST	NEED	WANT

DAILY LIFE *Planner*

DATES:

TODAY, *my primary goals are*

MOR   **AFT**   **EVE**

TODAY, *my primary goals are*

MOR   **AFT**   **EVE**

TODAY, *my primary goals are*

MOR   **AFT**   **EVE**

DAILY LIFE *Planner*

DATES:

TODAY, *my primary goals are*

MOR

AFT

EVE

TODAY, *my primary goals are*

MOR

AFT

EVE

TODAY, *my primary goals are*

MOR

AFT

EVE

DAILY LIFE *Planner*

DATES:

TODAY, *my primary goals are*

MOR

AFT

EVE

NOTES:

WEEKLY EXPENSE *Tracker*

DATES:

DESCRIPTION	CATEGORY	COST	NEED	WANT

DAILY LIFE *Planner*

DATES:

TODAY, *my primary goals are*

MOR

AFT

EVE

TODAY, *my primary goals are*

MOR

AFT

EVE

TODAY, *my primary goals are*

MOR

AFT

EVE

DAILY LIFE *Planner*

DATES:

TODAY, *my primary goals are*

(MOR)   (AFT)   (EVE)

TODAY, *my primary goals are*

(MOR)   (AFT)   (EVE)

TODAY, *my primary goals are*

(MOR)   (AFT)   (EVE)

DAILY LIFE *Planner*

DATES:

TODAY, *my primary goals are*

MOR

AFT

EVE

NOTES:

WEEKLY EXPENSE *Tracker*

DATES:

DESCRIPTION	CATEGORY	COST	NEED	WANT

DAILY LIFE *Planner*

DATES:

TODAY, *my primary goals are*

MOR

AFT

EVE

TODAY, *my primary goals are*

MOR

AFT

EVE

TODAY, *my primary goals are*

MOR

AFT

EVE

DAILY LIFE *Planner*

DATES:

TODAY, *my primary goals are*

MOR

AFT

EVE

TODAY, *my primary goals are*

MOR

AFT

EVE

TODAY, *my primary goals are*

MOR

AFT

EVE

DAILY LIFE *Planner*

DATES:

TODAY, *my primary goals are*

MOR	AFT	EVE

NOTES:

FINANCIAL *Journal*

MONTH 5

Date:_______________________

INCOME *Tracker*
- MONTHLY -

SOURCE	AMOUNT	M	T	W	T	F	S	S

ONE-TIME *Bills*

MONTH:

COMPANY:

ACCOUNT #:

PHONE#:

WEBSITE URL:

BILL DUE DATE:

ONLINE ACCOUNT INFORMATION: **USERNAME**   **PASSWORD**

BILL TOTAL:

COMPANY:

ACCOUNT #:

PHONE#:

WEBSITE URL:

BILL DUE DATE:

ONLINE ACCOUNT INFORMATION: **USERNAME**   **PASSWORD**

BILL TOTAL:

COMPANY:

ACCOUNT #:

PHONE#:

WEBSITE URL:

BILL DUE DATE:

ONLINE ACCOUNT INFORMATION: **USERNAME**   **PASSWORD**

BILL TOTAL:

NOTES

ONE-TIME *Bills*

MONTH:

COMPANY:

ACCOUNT #:   WEBSITE URL:

PHONE#:   BILL DUE DATE:

ONLINE ACCOUNT INFORMATION: **USERNAME**   **PASSWORD**

BILL TOTAL:

COMPANY:

ACCOUNT #:   WEBSITE URL:

PHONE#:   BILL DUE DATE:

ONLINE ACCOUNT INFORMATION: **USERNAME**   **PASSWORD**

BILL TOTAL:

COMPANY:

ACCOUNT #:   WEBSITE URL:

PHONE#:   BILL DUE DATE:

ONLINE ACCOUNT INFORMATION: **USERNAME**   **PASSWORD**

BILL TOTAL:

NOTES

WEEKLY EXPENSE *Tracker*

DATES:

DESCRIPTION	CATEGORY	COST		NEED	WANT

DAILY LIFE *Planner*

DATES:

TODAY, *my primary goals are*

MOR

AFT

EVE

TODAY, *my primary goals are*

MOR

AFT

EVE

TODAY, *my primary goals are*

MOR

AFT

EVE

DAILY LIFE *Planner*

DATES:

TODAY, *my primary goals are*

MOR

AFT

EVE

TODAY, *my primary goals are*

MOR

AFT

EVE

TODAY, *my primary goals are*

MOR

AFT

EVE

DAILY LIFE *Planner*

DATES:

TODAY, *my primary goals are*

MOR	AFT	EVE

NOTES:

WEEKLY EXPENSE *Tracker*

DATES:

DESCRIPTION	CATEGORY	COST	NEED	WANT

DAILY LIFE *Planner*

DATES:

TODAY, *my primary goals are*

MOR

AFT

EVE

TODAY, *my primary goals are*

MOR

AFT

EVE

TODAY, *my primary goals are*

MOR

AFT

EVE

DAILY LIFE *Planner*

DATES:

TODAY, *my primary goals are*

MOR | AFT | EVE

TODAY, *my primary goals are*

MOR | AFT | EVE

TODAY, *my primary goals are*

MOR | AFT | EVE

DAILY LIFE *Planner*

DATES:

TODAY, *my primary goals are*

MOR

AFT

EVE

NOTES:

WEEKLY EXPENSE *Tracker*

DATES:

DESCRIPTION	CATEGORY	COST	NEED	WANT

DAILY LIFE *Planner*

DATES:

TODAY, *my primary goals are*

MOR

AFT

EVE

TODAY, *my primary goals are*

MOR

AFT

EVE

TODAY, *my primary goals are*

MOR

AFT

EVE

DAILY LIFE *Planner*

DATES:

TODAY, *my primary goals are*

MOR

AFT

EVE

TODAY, *my primary goals are*

MOR

AFT

EVE

TODAY, *my primary goals are*

MOR

AFT

EVE

DAILY LIFE *Planner*

DATES:

TODAY, *my primary goals are*

MOR

AFT

EVE

NOTES:

WEEKLY EXPENSE *Tracker*

DATES:

DESCRIPTION	CATEGORY	COST	NEED	WANT

DAILY LIFE *Planner*

DATES:

TODAY, *my primary goals are*

MOR

AFT

EVE

TODAY, *my primary goals are*

MOR

AFT

EVE

TODAY, *my primary goals are*

MOR

AFT

EVE

DAILY LIFE *Planner*

DATES:

TODAY, *my primary goals are*

MOR

AFT

EVE

TODAY, *my primary goals are*

MOR

AFT

EVE

TODAY, *my primary goals are*

MOR

AFT

EVE

DAILY LIFE *Planner*

DATES:

TODAY, *my primary goals are*

MOR

AFT

EVE

NOTES:

FINANCIAL *Journal*

MONTH 6

Date:_______________________

INCOME *Tracker*
- MONTHLY -

SOURCE	AMOUNT	M	T	W	T	F	S	S

ONE-TIME *Bills*

MONTH:

COMPANY:

ACCOUNT #:
PHONE#:

WEBSITE URL:
BILL DUE DATE:

ONLINE ACCOUNT INFORMATION: **USERNAME**   **PASSWORD**

BILL TOTAL:

COMPANY:

ACCOUNT #:
PHONE#:

WEBSITE URL:
BILL DUE DATE:

ONLINE ACCOUNT INFORMATION   **USERNAME**   **PASSWORD**

BILL TOTAL:

COMPANY:

ACCOUNT #:
PHONE#:

WEBSITE URL:
BILL DUE DATE:

ONLINE ACCOUNT INFORMATION: **USERNAME**   **PASSWORD**

BILL TOTAL:

NOTES

ONE-TIME *Bills*

MONTH:

COMPANY:

ACCOUNT #:

PHONE#:

WEBSITE URL:

BILL DUE DATE:

ONLINE ACCOUNT INFORMATION: **USERNAME**   **PASSWORD**

BILL TOTAL:

COMPANY:

ACCOUNT #:

PHONE#:

WEBSITE URL:

BILL DUE DATE:

ONLINE ACCOUNT INFORMATION: **USERNAME**   **PASSWORD**

BILL TOTAL:

COMPANY:

ACCOUNT #:

PHONE#:

WEBSITE URL:

BILL DUE DATE:

ONLINE ACCOUNT INFORMATION: **USERNAME**   **PASSWORD**

BILL TOTAL:

NOTES

WEEKLY EXPENSE *Tracker*

DATES:

DESCRIPTION	CATEGORY	COST	NEED	WANT

DAILY LIFE *Planner*

DATES:

TODAY, *my primary goals are*

(MOR)   (AFT)   (EVE)

TODAY, *my primary goals are*

(MOR)   (AFT)   (EVE)

TODAY, *my primary goals are*

(MOR)   (AFT)   (EVE)

DAILY LIFE *Planner*

DATES:

TODAY, *my primary goals are*

MOR

AFT

EVE

TODAY, *my primary goals are*

MOR

AFT

EVE

TODAY, *my primary goals are*

MOR

AFT

EVE

DAILY LIFE *Planner*

DATES:

TODAY, *my primary goals are*

MOR

AFT

EVE

NOTES:

WEEKLY EXPENSE *Tracker*

DATES:

DESCRIPTION	CATEGORY	COST	NEED	WANT

DAILY LIFE *Planner*

DATES:

TODAY, *my primary goals are*

MOR

AFT

EVE

TODAY, *my primary goals are*

MOR

AFT

EVE

TODAY, *my primary goals are*

MOR

AFT

EVE

DAILY LIFE *Planner*

DATES:

TODAY, *my primary goals are*

MOR

AFT

EVE

TODAY, *my primary goals are*

MOR

AFT

EVE

TODAY, *my primary goals are*

MOR

AFT

EVE

DAILY LIFE *Planner*

DATES:

TODAY, *my primary goals are*

MOR

AFT

EVE

NOTES:

WEEKLY EXPENSE *Tracker*

DATES:

DESCRIPTION	CATEGORY	COST	NEED	WANT

DAILY LIFE *Planner*

DATES:

TODAY, *my primary goals are*

MOR

AFT

EVE

TODAY, *my primary goals are*

MOR

AFT

EVE

TODAY, *my primary goals are*

MOR

AFT

EVE

DAILY LIFE *Planner*

DATES:

TODAY, *my primary goals are*

MOR

AFT

EVE

TODAY, *my primary goals are*

MOR

AFT

EVE

TODAY, *my primary goals are*

MOR

AFT

EVE

DAILY LIFE *Planner*

DATES:

TODAY, *my primary goals are*

MOR

AFT

EVE

NOTES:

WEEKLY EXPENSE *Tracker*

DATES:

DESCRIPTION	CATEGORY	COST	NEED	WANT

DAILY LIFE *Planner*

DATES:

TODAY, *my primary goals are*

MOR

AFT

EVE

TODAY, *my primary goals are*

MOR

AFT

EVE

TODAY, *my primary goals are*

MOR

AFT

EVE

DAILY LIFE *Planner*

DATES:

TODAY, *my primary goals are*

MOR　　　　　　　　AFT　　　　　　　　EVE

TODAY, *my primary goals are*

MOR　　　　　　　　AFT　　　　　　　　EVE

TODAY, *my primary goals are*

MOR　　　　　　　　AFT　　　　　　　　EVE

DAILY LIFE *Planner*

DATES:

TODAY, *my primary goals are*

MOR

AFT

EVE

NOTES:

FINANCIAL *Journal*